Woofs of Wisdom

A collection of Dog Training and
Behaviour Soundbites

Tony Cruse

Publishing Notes

Credits

Produced, compiled and edited by Tony Cruse

Cover Concept by Tony Cruse

Cover artwork and all Illustrations by Denise O'Moore

Photos by Carolyn Clarke

Typesetting by www.bookclaw.com

Formatting by www.bookclaw.com

Contributors

Andrea Arden, Anna Patfield, Annie Phenix, Carolyn Menteith, Claudia Estanislau, David Ryan, Dawn Antoniak-Mitchell, Denise Armstrong, Denise Fenzi, Diane Kasperowicz, Donna Saunders, Dr Ian Dunbar, Grisha Stewart, Hannah Wilkinson, Isla Fishburn, Jacqueline Boyd, Jane Arden, Jane Williams, Jean Donaldson, Jo Pay, Justine Schuurmans, Karen Bush, Kay Attwood, Kay Laurence, Kelly Gorman Dunbar, Kirsten Dillon, Lily Clark, Linda Case, Linda Michaels, Lisa Tenzin-Dolma, Louise Glazebrook, Louise Wilson, Lynda Taylor, Mik Moeller, Muriel Brasseur, Sally Marchant, Sarah Fisher, Silvia Trkman, Sue Kinchin, Susan G Friedman, Suzanne Clothier, Theresa McKeon, Tim Bleecker, Toni Shelbourne, Tony Cruse, Tracie Hotchner and Val Harvey.

Introduction

A dog's life is relatively simple. They sleep, they play, they eat and eat some more and sleep again. However, to fully appreciate our pet dogs and their ways, we can look further. This book is based on scientific knowledge but written in a clear and concise way. My primary objective was to present a book of short, useful phrases of which can be easily understood. Each 'Woof of Wisdom' can help the relationship with your dog and assist your understanding as to why dogs do what they do.

If you share your life with a pet dog, you are your dog's trainer! Woofs of Wisdom is aimed at pet dog owners, dog enthusiasts, dog trainers, professionals and all interested in canine behaviour and learning. This paperback is designed to be neat and portable because you just never know when you may be in need of wisdom!

I have been attending workshops and seminars presented by canine and animal experts for many years and like most keen students, I would take a notebook and pen. Hey, never stop being a student! Plenty of notes were scribbled but I also jotted down short soundbites which the speaker may have said. It's these phrases that really stuck in my brain and these 'sticky' soundbites which have certainly helped me during my canine career.

After reviewing my notes, the short phrases and sentences were neatly written into a little pocketbook. And so the idea of this very book was born! Why keep them to myself? For the sake of all pet dogs...let's share this wonderful information and put it across so that it is understandable and sensible.

To create 'Woofs of Wisdom', I contacted over forty experts in the field of dog training, dog behaviour and animal psychology and asked for a short phrase which can help in pet dog training and behaviour. The canine world is generally a friendly bubble to work in and I wholeheartedly thank each contributor for jumping on-board and making Woofs of Wisdom such an exciting project.

Each 'woof of wisdom' is not necessarily a direct quote. Many contributions are unique phrases, whilst others are common knowledge in the dog behaviour world. We all want to share this wonderful knowledge to help dogs and their owners. As the creator of Woofs of Wisdom, I wanted to keep each contributor's explanation as original as possible therefore I have performed very little editing. Also, the contributor's native spelling remains but this does not spoil the flow of information.

There are 91 Woofs of Wisdom and each one is numbered. After each phrase, there is a brief explanation before the contributor's details. Please check out the Woofs of Wisdom expert contributors. They all have some great knowledge to offer the canine, animal and teaching world.

Finally, my deepest respect and gratitude goes out to my friends and colleagues who have contributed to Woofs of Wisdom......Andrea Arden, Anna Patfield, Annie Phenix, Carolyn Menteith, Claudia Estanislau, David Ryan, Dawn Antoniak-Mitchell, Denise Armstrong, Denise Fenzi, Diane Kasperowicz, Donna Saunders, Dr Ian Dunbar, Grisha Stewart, Hannah Wilkinson, Isla Fishburn, Jacqueline Boyd, Jane Arden, Jane Williams, Jean Donaldson, Jo Pay, Justine Schuurmans, Karen Bush, Kay Attwood, Kay Laurence, Kelly Gorman Dunbar, Kirsten Dillon, Lily Clark, Linda Case, Linda Michaels, Lisa Tenzin-Dolma, Louise Glazebrook, Louise Wilson, Lynda Taylor, Mik Moeller, Muriel Brasseur, Sally Marchant, Sarah Fisher, Silvia Trkman, Sue Kinchin, Susan G Friedman,

Suzanne Clothier, Theresa McKeon, Tim Bleecker, Toni Shelbourne, Tracie Hotchner and Val Harvey.

With 91 contributions, which is your favourite Woof?

Woofs and Smiles,

Tony Cruse

Learning is a combination of repetition and association

– Tony Cruse

Tony explains

This common phrase describes how all species learn. For our dogs, if each task is made rewarding and successfully rewarded...learning will occur. 'Hey if I put my bottom on the floor when you say sit, I get a biscuit!" He knows because it is the fifth time it has occurred today. Learning is happening.

A history of good associations needs to be established, so the dog is more likely to repeat it next time. However, if a dog is only taught to sit in the kitchen, he may not sit by the kerb side. Repeat each exercise often, in many locations... and keep it rewarding!

More about Tony

Tony Cruse is a full-time dog trainer who also advises on a variety of canine problem behaviours. He is a regular feature writer for various magazines and a sort-after speaker. Tony is the creator of this book and his last book was the highly regarded, '101 Doggy Dilemmas'. www.tc-dog-training.co.uk

Catch your dog in the act of doing something right. And PRAISE!

– Dr. Ian Dunbar

Ian Explains

Most people suffer the disastrous foible of ignoring dogs when they are good and only responding when they are "bad". Some dogs (and many children) will misbehave on purpose just to get attention. Even bad attention is better than none. Be representative with your feedback. Every five minutes praise and gently pet your dog for good behavior and you'll have a different dog by day's end.

More about Ian

Dr. Ian Dunbar is a veterinarian, animal behaviourist, dog trainer, author, lecturer, skier, gardener and Arsenal, Yorkshire and Warriors supporter. After retiring from the seminar trail (nine months a year in hotels), Dr. Dunbar now lectures online at DunbarAcademy.com and occasionally blogs and vlogs at DogStarDaily.com

Unlabel Me

- Susan G Friedman

Susan Explains

Bad dog. Shy dog. Fearful dog. Labels like these don't help us help dogs because they don't describe what we really need to know -- what the dog is actually doing and what's going on when the dog does it! Labels are just concepts so they can't really cause anything. Wouldn't we all benefit from being unlabeled?

More about Susan

Dr. Friedman is a retired psychology professor who consults with animal caregivers around the world. She disseminates the science of behavior change and its effective, humane teaching technology, applied behavior analysis. Her website has articles, posters and other media (including translations), which is available for downloading, free of charge. www.behaviorworks.org

*Remember your side
of the contract*

– Val Harvey

Val Explains

One of the most common training issues that I see is that of loose lead walking. We don't want our dog to pull on the lead when we are out on a walk. That's obvious. But what do a lot of people do when their dog pulls? They pull him back. Many dogs think this is how they walk – he pulls, you pull, he pulls, you... well, you get the idea. So, if you want your dog to understand that he shouldn't pull, remember that you shouldn't pull him either! If he pulls, stand still, wait for the lead to loosen, then ask him to return to your side and reward him. Walk on, if the lead is loose, reward him (often to start with). If the lead tightens, stop, wait, but don't pull him back. That is the contract. Honour it and soon your dog will too.

More about Val

Val has been helping people to train their dogs for more than twenty years. She is a member of APDT, UK whose members coach owners to train their dogs using kind, fair and effective methods. Members can be found on www.apdt.co.uk

Be Proactive not Reactive

- Jane Ardern

Jane Explains

When getting a puppy look for all the things you like, capture and reward them. Don't wait till things go wrong and then try to fix them. Reward the right things first and they will stick around. The 'problem' behaviours are then less likely to develop.

Things to reward your dog for...
Sitting, relaxing, waiting patiently, being quiet, watching and turning away from distractions, following you, listening to you, checking-in on you.

Reward with a mix of all the things that motivate a puppy. These are food, attention, affection and play.

More about Jane

Jane Ardern BSc (Hons) Speaker, Trainer, Spaniel Specialist
Kennel Club Dog Trainer of the Year 2015
Breeder at Riverirk Working Cocker Spaniels
Online Positive Dog Training
www.clickertrainer.co.uk

Play to stay!

- Donna Saunders

Donna Explains

Use fun stuff such as toys and play to encourage your dog to create and build a strong bond with you that helps to make *you* the best place to be. This is 'super useful' for many situations such as recalls and emergency situations!

More about Donna

Donna owns In The Doghouse Pet Lodge & amp; Training Centre in Spain & has many hats! Working with dogs for 11 years, Donna has picked up amongst others, City & Guilds, IMDT & FitPaws accreditations along her journey.
www.inthedoghousedtc.com

Sometimes you win.
Sometimes you learn.

– Silvia Trkman

Silvia Explains

Failures are just as important as successes. Perhaps more so. They give focus to your training, show what could still be better and give you an opportunity to grow and improve. Perceive every failure as a new challenge and every challenge as just another fun training opportunity. Things would be way too boring if perfect.

More about Silvia

For the past 20 years, Silvia Trkman has been one of the most successful agility competitors and trainers, winning World, European and National Championships many times with various dogs. See www.lolabuland.com

You are what you eat – probably!

- Anna Patfield

Anna Explains

We talk about 'brain food', but essentially everything that we eat is used to power the body and brain. Everything from plates of meat to tiny vitamin pills plays a part in moving chemicals around the body. It amazes me how we actually survive given how bad our diets can be! The same is true for our dogs.

There are of course many genetic and environmental factors that influence health and behaviour but a healthy balanced diet also plays its part.

Therefore, no matter how you choose to feed your dog, please ensure that the diet is nutritionally balanced and suitable for their individual needs. Home-prepared foods should follow carefully devised recipes. Manufactured foods should not have lots of extras added: the recipe is already nutritionally balanced.

And remember that your dog is an individual - what suits one may not be right for another.

More about Anna

Anna is a fully qualified and experienced dog behaviourist with a passion for unravelling the mysteries surrounding behaviour and behavioural nutrition. She can help you to get inside your dog's mind and to really understand what makes them tick.

PawsAbility.co.uk

TheGoodDogDiet.com.

Having choice is
reinforcing, having too
much choice is paralysing

– Kay Laurence

Kay Explains

Learning to choose is a puzzle solving skill that can take a lifetime to learn. Choice is best served within a framework. We are going for a walk together, when we cross the road there is no choice and you need to walk at my side, but when we walk along the hedge you can choose to stop and sniff and I will wait for you and keep you safe. But you cannot choose to sniff the whole of the forest without me. A limited choice is perfect.

More about Kay

Kay Laurence
Sharing life managed by collies in a style demanded by Gordon Setters.
Innovative and effective teaching by learning about dogs. Training based on science and understanding, delivered with experience and empathy, reinforced from the heart with passion, joy and enthusiasm.
Learningaboutdogs.com

Set your dog up to succeed

- Louise Glazebrook

Louise Explains

Many owners focus on the one behaviour their dog isn't performing well, whilst ignoring the huge list of things they are brilliant at. It's really important to not lose sight of these as you can create a vicious circle of disappointment and negativity.

I want my clients and their dogs to enjoy being together, so they make time to do things they know their dog loves and are really good at. Focus on the great many things your dog brings to your life and when you have to work on that one tricky thing, it won't seem such a mountain to climb. Your relationship will also benefit hugely, which in turn will bring you on leaps and jumps when working together.

More about Louise

Louise Glazebrook, dog behaviourist and trainer, founder of The Darling Dog Company in London, UK. Working to help dogs and their owners live happily together. Louise regularly appears on BBC TV. www.thedarlingdogcompany.co.uk

Don't Recall, Refuel

- Toni Shelbourne

Toni Explains

Refuel your dog's curiosity by doing fun imaginative things to encourage engagement, and improve recall at the same time. Get your dog to think, 'Wow, what's going to happen this time when she calls me?'. 'She may have found a fabulous treat in the grass, she's a really good forager and always shares her finds'. 'Or maybe she will throw a treat or toy in any direction, I'd better rush back'. Be the most fun ever and recall will no longer be a chore for you and your dog.

More about Toni

Toni Shelbourne has worked professionally with dogs since 1989. She is a Tellington TTouch Practitioner, Real Dog Yoga Instructor and Author. Visit www.tonishelbourne.co.uk to find out more. For the 'HELP! My Dog...' book series, visit the Facebook page. Canine EBooks by Toni Shelbourne & Karen Bush (Also available in paperback).

Pat, pet, pause

- Justine Schuurmans

Justine Explains

This is a reminder of how to pet a dog in a way that
a) Gives the dog a choice
AND
b) he can enjoy too!

First, PAT your leg to invite the dog over
If he approaches – you're good to PET.
Then PAUSE for 3 seconds to see if he wants more.

More about Justine

Justine Schuurmans is the owner of The Family Dog, an online training company for the WHOLE family.

The company's fun, music-based videos for kids have quickly become the trademark of all their online programs. With in-school training programs and an international bite prevention campaign, the company's mission is to help families worldwide live happily and safely with their dogs.
www.thefamilydog.com

Changing the underlying emotion changes the behaviour

- David Ryan

David Explains

Behaviours are driven by emotions. The dog feels a certain way and acts accordingly. If we think the way the dog is acting is inappropriate, the ideal way to change the behaviour is to change the emotion underpinning it. When we change the emotion, the dog feels differently about the situation and therefore behaves differently.

More about David

David Ryan has written four books, including and Dogs that Bite and Fight and another on Predatory Chase. He currently works with local and national charities rehoming 'difficult' dogs and provides a legal expert witness consultancy on canine behaviour. www.dog-secrets.co.uk

Dogs do what works

- Linda Case

Linda Explains

This is the basic underlying premise of operant learning; the consequences of behavior influence a dog's future behavior. Dogs continue to offer behaviors that "pay off" in terms of pleasurable consequences - attaining or maintaining access to something that they enjoy. It is not about "knowing what is wrong or right" (i.e. your dog does not care that you consider it poor manners to jump on counters or steal food) - it is about what behaviors lead to enjoyable consequences. Manage the setting, change the motivation, and alter the consequences to change "what works" if you do not like a behavior that your dog is offering!

More about Linda

Linda Case is a dog trainer, canine nutritionist and science writer. She owns AutumnGold Consulting and Dog Training Center located in central Illinois, USA. Linda is the author of seven dog books and "The Science Dog" blog.
www.thesciencedog.wordpress.com

Distance is your friend

- Tony Cruse

Tony Explains

An important phrase used by many professionals when helping and training anxious dogs. Dogs are exceptionally aware of social distance and similar to a magnet, the closer the dog is to the trigger of the behaviour, the more intense the behaviour. If a worried dog is close to another dog, his barking and lunging may be more severe. Calmly moving him away to a comfortable distance can ease the unwanted reactions and help the dog feel a little better about the trigger (e.g. other dog).

This doesn't have to be forever because distance can be used to help the dog within his comfort zone (at a distance). Good things happen when the trigger is in view. Having built up a positive association with the trigger in sight, over time the distance can be gently and slowly decreased.

More about Tony

Tony Cruse is a full-time dog trainer who also advises on a variety of canine problem behaviours. Tony runs classes and has completed over 900 behaviour and training consultations. He is also is a nominated lecturer for Writtle College University, UK.
www.tc-dog-training.co.uk

No one is perfect!

- Lily Clark

Lily Explains

All people have days full of stress and frustration which can shorten our fuses with our pets. Our dogs can have difficult days too. Your dog forgives you! The best way to make up with your dog and resolve the conflict is to play a fun game with them; get involved!

Anyone who says they have a perfect dog is lying and it is frankly unacceptable and delusional for anyone to portray that a dog has to be 100% perfectly behaved and bombproof. Dogs are thinking, feeling creatures with a mind of their own. We can only guide them in the best way we can using our current level of knowledge. So educate yourself in what your dog is trying to tell you. All dogs speak with their body, so be one of those people who know how to listen.

More about Lily

Lily created Suppawt as a bespoke service providing realistic training for normal people and normal dogs. Lily specializes in rehabilitating rescue and reactive dogs.
BSc Hons Animal Behaviour, APDT
www.suppawt.com

It's okay if you occasionally dig a hole when you train; the trick is to stop digging before you have a grave

– Denise Fenzi

Denise Explains

We all make mistakes in training. This is equally true for the experienced trainer and the total novice alike; the difference is what happens next. Experienced trainers recognize when their plan isn't working and they change direction. They stop, regroup, create a new plan and try again! There is no shame in making an error because it's all part of the learning process. But if you insist on heading down a path that is not working for you, then you can end up with a really unhappy, stressed and confused dog and that situation is much harder to remedy.

Don't worry about ending on a high or a low note; simply quit when you recognize it's time. And when you see you're digging a hole? It's definitely time to quit!!

More about Denise

Denise is a professional dog trainer who specializes in motivation and preparing dog sports teams for competition using no-force training methods. Her books can be found on Amazon worldwide. Denise's online school can be found at www.fenzidogsportsacademy.com

If in doubt, say, "Sit"

- Dr. Ian Dunbar

Ian Explains

A prompt sit and reliable stay prevents or stops over 90% of behavior and training problems. Sit is the simplest response to teach and if a dog is sitting, it can not jump up, dash out the front door, lunge on leash, chase its tail, chase rabbits, slap children in the face with a waggy tail, use your living room as an Agility Course, jump the cat, or hump your Great Aunt's knee.

Whenever your puppy/dog misbehaves, there is no need to cause fear or pain, simply calmly and quietly instruct your dog how you would like it to act, for example, to Sit.

More about Ian

Dr. Ian Dunbar is a veterinarian, animal behaviourist, dog trainer, author, lecturer, skier, gardener and Arsenal, Yorkshire and Warriors supporter. After retiring from the seminar trail (nine months a year in hotels), Dr. Dunbar now lectures online at DunbarAcademy.com and occasionally blogs and vlogs at DogStarDaily.com

Every behaviour is a cheesecake

- Kirsten Dillon

Kirsten Explains

Every time we identify a behaviour we would like to change, we should remember that the reason or motivation for the behaviour will rarely have one pure cause.

Think of the behaviour like a cheesecake and the causes as individual slices. Let's take, barking at other dogs – whilst one 'reason slice' could be enormous, i.e. poor early socialisation, there WILL be further 'slices' such as genetics, fear, habit, frustration, reinforcement history (effectiveness) etc.

We can reasonably identify individual slices by gaining a good history and once we've done this, it becomes easier to understand and begin an effective change. For example, we can address the 'habit slice', the 'reinforcement slice', and the 'frustration slice' simply by avoiding the opportunity to practice. Instantly we've reduced the size of the cheesecake and can focus on the remaining slice, poor socialisation, with less affecting or distracting factors.

More about Kirsten

Kirsten Dillon is a dog trainer and behaviourist, working in Surrey and London, UK. She is also Head of Training at the charity Veterans With Dogs and a Trainer and Assessor for Dog AID (Assistance In Disability)
www.kdcaninespecialist.com

Next time someone tells you your dog is really a wolf. Throw them a banana!

– Tim Bleecker

Tim Explains

If more time was spent building trust and training the domesticated dog, the less time could be spent worrying about whether the 'wolf' in the house is trying to 'claim the sofa'.
The idea that watching wolf behaviour will give you answers to everyday problems is the same as popping down to the zoo to observe the chimps in order to deal with your partner's unwanted behaviour.

More about Tim

Tim runs classes in Nottingham/Mansfield, UK and carries out 1-2-1 sessions assisting owners with behavioural issues.
He takes a special interest in helping owners understand and deal with dog-to-dog aggression.

Tim is a full member of the
Association of Pet Dog Trainers, (APDT UK)

www.nottinghamdogtrainer.co.uk
www.mansfielddogtraining.co.uk

You have a contract with this dog, for the life of this dog

– Kay Laurence

Kay Explains

Strangers do not have a right to touch your dog, say hello, or judge you. No more than you would let a stranger touch your child, give them sweets or advise you on their well being. We want our dogs to learn who are friends, who are acquaintances and who should be ignored. This starts on the first day with your puppy when you start your contract of care and lifetime of companionship. Your dog is always more important than the desires of a passing stranger.

More about Kay

Kay Laurence
Sharing life managed by collies in a style demanded by Gordon Setters.
Innovative and effective teaching by learning about dogs. Training based on science and understanding, delivered with experience and empathy, reinforced from the heart with passion, joy and enthusiasm.
Learningaboutdogs.com

Train at the dog's pace rather than what you want or think it should be

– Denise Armstrong

Denise Explains

Training is a roller coaster of highs and lows and for our dogs to reach the end goal, we must accommodate the speed at which they learn. Make it easy to train and measure progress by training in incremental steps, changing only one criterion at a time, i.e. distance OR distraction - not both at the same time. Otherwise, how will you OR the dog know which part of the training is going right or wrong?
Sometimes we have to take a step back to rebuild previous training, it's quality over quantity that counts and not a competition to race to the finish.

More about Denise

Denise is highly qualified, experienced and passionate about building partnerships on the rewarding road to success. She excels at coaching owners to navigate life's' unexpected speed bumps and provides the guidance needed when a roadblock problem appears in the way of progress.
www.reddogtraining.co.uk

Teach DON'T Test!

- Justine Schuurmans

Justine Explains

So many families (all human beings) want results fast! They're often in a hurry to drop the reward during training and 'see' if the dog has acquired the skill WAY too early.

'Teach DON'T Test' is a reminder to keep up with the reward schedule to ensure they get the success they're looking for in the longterm.

More about Justine

Justine Schuurmans is the owner of The Family Dog, an online training company for the WHOLE family.

The company's fun, music-based videos for kids have quickly become the trademark of all their online programs. With in-school training programs and an international bite prevention campaign, the company's mission is to help families worldwide live happily and safely with their dogs.
www.thefamilydog.com

Buffer Time!!

- Tony Cruse

Tony Explains

Our dogs don't cope well with sudden changes in the environment. Many owners expect dogs to 'deal with it'. They often don't and that's when we see a dog that is out of control. Barking, jumping-up and chewing are all doggy coping mechanisms. Examples are visiting new locations, arriving at the park and visitors. Does your dog calmly cope?

You can help your dog to 'acclimatise' to these changes and environments by adding 'Buffer Time'! Buffer Time is the short period of time which can act as a buffer between the chaos and the calm. Arrive at the park...buffer time in the car...now commence the walk! A visitor arrives at home...buffer time in the kitchen...now introduce the visitor. Arrive early at the training class...buffer time in the car park...now begin the lesson. 'Buffer time' is breathing time!

More about Tony

Tony Cruse is a full-time dog trainer who also advises on a variety of canine problem behaviours. He has completed over 900 training and behaviour consultations. Tony is also a writer and a sought-after speaker.
Tony is the producer of this very book.
www.tc-dog-training.co.uk

Outcomes are the purpose for behaving

– Susan Friedman

Susan Explains

Our eyes are to see, ears are to hear, and legs are to run. Our behavior is to produce outcomes from the environment. Good outcomes strengthen behavior; poor outcomes weaken behavior. Provide good outcomes more!

More about Susan

Dr. Friedman is a retired psychology professor who consults with animal caregivers around the world. She disseminates the science of behavior change and its effective, humane teaching technology, applied behavior analysis. Her website has articles, posters and other media (including translations), which is available for downloading, free of charge. www.behaviorworks.org

Leave your ego at the door

- Muriel Brasseur

Muriel Explains

Undoubtedly, this is THE biggest lesson I have learned from a lifetime within animal behaviour and training. The moment you start to work with a dog and its human(s), it has to stop being about you. If you're in it to look good and pose with dogs to feed your self-esteem, be popular on social media and become a star, or because you like telling people what to do and dazzle clients with your knowledge and skills, how much use are you really going to be? Eventually, if you are worth your salt, one dog followed by many will come along to deconstruct you and teach you humility. Ultimately, it's about service and striving to be the best person you can be to help better the lives of dogs and their carers.

More about Muriel

BSc (Hons), PhD, PACT-KSA
Director of the Professional Association of Canine Trainers (PACT)
Lecturer in Companion Animal Behaviour at the University of Oxford
www.pact-dogs.com

"How is this for you?"

– Suzanne Clothier

Suzanne Explains

This is one of my six Elemental Questions(TM), and the one that needs to be constantly asked. I keep the relationship central to all I do with any dog, so I am always concerned with how the dog is experiencing any given moment. I don't want the dog unhappy, confused, afraid, anxious, frustrated, annoyed or angry. By asking, "How is this for you?" I keep myself open to really listening to the dog and observing his experience. If things aren't right, I make changes immediately. This keeps things from going wrong.

Despite good intentions, if we don't ask this simple question, we may miss the dog's experience, focusing on what *we* want or intend. When we really *see the dog* and hear the answers the dog can give, we are on the path for humane, ethical training and developing the strong, healthy relationships we all want with our dogs.

More about Suzanne

Trainer Suzanne Clothier's Relationship Centered Training (RCT) approach has helped countless dogs worldwide with her innovative, humane techniques. The author of the highly regarded "Bones Would Rain from the Sky", she has developed a broad range of programs for dog lovers, trainers & organizations (CARAT, RAT, FAT, Enriched Puppy). https://www.suzanneclothier.com

Trust is a gift that we earn

- Lisa Tenzin-Dolma

Lisa Explains

Trust can take time to develop. Our dogs gradually learn that we're worthy of their trust and they respond in kind when we treat them with understanding and compassion. This creates the foundation for a harmonious relationship.

We earn trust when we take the time and make the effort to build a relationship. Trust comes naturally when we're consistent in our responses and when we reward the behaviours we want to encourage and pre-empt behaviours we wish to discourage so that opportunities to rehearse these don't arise. Our dogs feel safe and secure when they understand what is expected of them.

More about Lisa

Lisa Tenzin-Dolma is founder and principal of The International School for Canine Psychology & Behaviour, founder of The Dog Welfare Alliance, co-chair of The Association of INTODogs, and represents INTODogs within the Animal Behaviour & Training Council. Her 33 published books include 5 books on dog behaviour. www.theiscp.com

There is no free lunch: no motivation, no training

- Jean Donaldson

Jean Explains

Dog guardians have been misled for generations about the need to concretely motivate their dogs. Unscrupulous trainers prey on this with promises of compliance and good behavior provided the owner displays "leadership" or some sort of right "energy." If you watch what such trainers actually do, they motivate concretely like everybody else. They may elect hazing, pain and intimidation, but they motivate in the physical world.

More about Jean

Jean Donaldson, founder and Director of The Academy for Dog Trainers, and author of The Culture Clash.

www.academyfordogtrainers.com

Conservation Makes Scents

- Louise Wilson

Louise Explains

With many years experience training detection dogs for law enforcement, police, Government agents and more- when I get asked - why use sniffer dogs for conservation? - this quote is perfect- 'Conservation Makes Scents'!

More about Louise

Founder of Conservation K9 Consultancy- leaders in wildlife monitoring, wildlife crime detection in the UK and worldwide using Detection Dogs. Louise has vast experience in this area in the UK and a robust worldwide work portfolio.
Www.conservationk9consultancy.com

Dogs Have Emotions Too!

- Linda Michaels, MA Psychology

Linda Explains

Darwin theorized as far back as 1872 that animals have emotions but sadly society has been disappointingly and often passionately resistant in accepting the truth about our dog's emotions. Research now demonstrates dog's emotions are similar, although possibly not as nuanced, as our own. Leaders in the research field such as Dr. Panksepp, the renowned neuroscientist, Dr. Marc Bekoff, Psychology Today, and Dr. Adam Miklosi's, stunning evidentiary MRI studies, make it clear that dogs have many similar emotions. Dogs hurt. Dogs feel pain. Dogs feel fear. Dogs feel joy.

Although corporate, scientific and training industry interests may find it profitable to NOT recognize dog emotions, our long-suffering pets cannot speak for themselves and have a bottomless pit of unconditional love. This has allowed them to become targets of abuse. We ought to be protecting them. They deserve no less. Finally, this cannot be reasonably denied.

More about Linda
Linda Michaels, M.A., Psychology, author of "Do No Harm" Dog Training, is the creator of the HierarchyOfDogNeeds.com infographic used by veterinary behaviorists and force-free trainers. Linda's research experience in behavioral neurobiology makes her an expert in training aggressive dogs, puppies and wolfdogs in the Del Mar, CA area of the USA. DogPsychologistOnCall.com

Naughty is Normal

- Tony Cruse

Tony Explains

This is a common short, fun phrase which sums up puppyhood! Dogs are born not knowing our boundaries and expectations. The behaviour we consider naughty is simply a young animal finding out what works for him and what doesn't!

It is up to us, as owners, to reward the behaviour we consider normal (and acceptable). For example, jumping up may be considered naughty, but it's probably a dog trying to effectively greet a human just as dogs meeting dogs do, face to face. We can teach a dog that greeting and keeping his 'four paws on the floor' pays off. If he remains on the floor, he gets a big floor-level fuss and possibly a treat.

More about Tony

Tony Cruse is a full-time dog trainer who also advises on a variety of canine problem behaviours. He is a regular feature writer for various magazines and is part of the expert panel for the UK's Your Dog Magazine.
Tony is the producer of this very book.
www.tc-dog-training.co.uk

Be patient, persistent, consistent, and realistic with your training expectations and understand that the breed instincts in any dog can be modified, but never completely eliminated

– Dawn Antoniak-Mitchell, Esq.
CPDT-KSA, CBCC-KA

Dawn Explains

By learning about the work your dog's breed was originally developed to do, it will be easier to understand why he behaves the way he does. Unacceptable behaviors don't happen because your dog is dumb or mean; they happen because your dog is just that - a dog - behaving in a way that is influenced, in part, by his breed's instincts.

If you learn how to work with your dog's breed instincts, you can manage your dog proactively to prevent some breed-based problems from developing in the first place and develop a fair, effective training program to modify unacceptable behaviors which may have already started.

When you appreciate your dog for who he is at heart and the breed instincts and unique personality that influence his behavior, training will become a positive and productive journey you take together. You can then truly unleash your dog's potential!

More about Dawn

Dawn has been training people and dogs for over twenty-five years. She has written several breed-focused training books, including the award-winning "Teach Your Herding Breed to be a Great Companion Dog: From Obsessive to Outstanding." She owns BonaFide Dog Academy in Omaha, NE, USA.
www.bonafidedogacademy.com

Management and
motivation based training
are essential partners for
raising a happy and
mannerly dog

- Andrea Arden

Andrea Explains

By employing good management, pet parents can prevent the practice of undesirable behaviors and responses. In this way, they are setting their dog up for success by funnelling behavior in the right direction. Management prevents the practice of unwanted behaviors and frees up time and energy for turning the process of teaching desirable behaviors and responses into a fun and effective game that the dog is eager to be a part of. For example, step on the leash to prevent jumping up while at the same time rewarding the dog for keeping four paws on the floor when greeting people. Eventually, polite greetings will become strong and reliable and the use of management can be faded out.

More about Andrea

Andrea has been a family dog trainer for almost 25 years. She is the author of numerous books, including "Dog-Friendly Dog Training," and "Barron's Dog Training Bible." Andrea is a pet expert for The Today Show, Live with Kelly and Animal Planet. www.andreaarden.com

Ask the dog!

– Claudia Estanislau

Claudia Explains

When you are doing something with your dog, make sure it is with him and not to him! Is he compliant? So, to avoid doing something to him, just ask him. Be it grooming, a cuddle or running beside your bike, make sure your dog really wants to do it. How to ask? Here is an example, if you stroke your dog, then stop and wait for your dog to let you know if he wants more. He will either approach or avoid. Remember just ask the dog!

More about Claudia

Claudia Estanislau has been a force-free trainer over 10 years. She lives in Portugal where she runs her business. 'It's All About Dogs' where she teaches classes and addresses behaviour modification. She also teaches international seminars every year. www.itsallaboutdogs.org

All dogs are entitled to
growl and walk away

- David Ryan

David Explains

Growling is a reflection of an underlying emotion, whether that be fear or frustration. Walking away means they are dealing with it - they are communicating that they are upset but want to take it no further. If you stop dogs from growling, they may jump straight to a higher level of communication, such as biting without warning.

However, if a dog is frequently growling it shows that they are not happy and the reasons should be investigated so that the underlying problem can be addressed.

More about David

David Ryan has written four books, including and 'Dogs that Bite and Fight' and another on Predatory Chase. He currently works with local and national charities rehoming 'difficult' dogs and provides a legal expert witness consultancy on canine behaviour www.dog-secrets.co.uk

Be a giver, not a taker

- Tony Cruse

Tony Explains

This is a common phrase regarding dogs who guard food or items. Puppies often learn to compete for things which they consider valuable. The old advice was to teach the puppy not to guard by removing his meal bowl or his tasty bone. This can lead to a dog feeling more insecure around his food. The approaching person can then be seen as the problem! Can you imagine somebody removing your favourite meal when you are chowing down? Grrrr, indeed!!

We can teach a puppy to feel secure around food by 'giving and not taking'. For example, walk past his empty food bowl and drop in a piece of his meal. When he's finished it, repeat. It's win/win because you soon start becoming the predictor of good things and he eats happily without a perceived threat. If you really have to remove something; be smart and make an exchange.

More about Tony

Tony Cruse is a full-time dog trainer who also advises on a variety of canine problem behaviours. He has completed over 900 training and behaviour consultations. Tony is also a writer and a sought-after speaker.
He is the producer of this very book.
www.tc-dog-training.co.uk

Manage the environment, not the dog

- Grisha Stewart

Grisha Explains

For me, an ideal education teaches students to figure out how to handle various situations without having to be told. This applies to dogs, too, but we can't expect that to happen right away, with all the distractions out there.

Smart trainers set things up so that the dog is very likely to make great choices without needing to be cued by a person. Gradually make the environment more challenging - just enough to present the dog with a choice but similar enough to a familiar situation that the dog is still successful. With practice, your dog's choices become a solid habit.

This approach works as well for aggression and fear as it does for basic life skills like polite greetings. It may take more patience and creativity than being directive, but it definitely pays off in the long run when your dog makes great choices on his own!

More about Grisha

Grisha Stewart, MA, CPDT-KA specializes in canine social skills. She developed Behavior Adjustment Training (BAT) for puppy socialization and the rehabilitation of aggression, frustration, and fear. Grisha's books, streaming videos, DVDs, custom leashes, and online dog training school are available at GrishaStewart.com.

When co-existing with a dog,
we sign an unwritten contract
with nature; to provide a life
that promotes health,
longevity and wellness for our
canine friend

– Isla Fishburn

Isla Explains

Our dogs are more than just physical beings. They are emotional animals that are influenced by every experience - everything they see, hear, taste, smell, touch and feel. These very experiences can create imbalance(s) within the dog. This can cause physical, emotional, physiological, energetic and spiritual disharmony and affect your dog's health and longevity.

The subject of wellness covers many topics but all are equally important for our dogs to remain balanced, happy and content.

By inviting a dog into our homes, it is our duty as their human guardian(s) to learn all that we can to provide them with a long, healthy and balanced life. A life where they feel safe, a life where they can succeed, a life where they can learn calmly and a life that allows them to be the species, Canine, that they are.

More about Isla

Dr Fishburn has had a long interest in nature, healing and conservation. After spending several years with captive wolves and learning more about wellness, Isla began to observe the many distresses that domestic dogs experience. Isla created Kachina Canine to provide support for dogs and to educate their human guardians. www.kachinacanine.com

Dog Tired? Allow a
waking dog to sleep, rest
and doze

– Diane Kasperowicz

Diane Explains

Dogs require, on average, 12-14 hours of sleep per day. However, puppies need much longer requiring an average of 18-20 hours. Puppies who expend a lot of energy and who are always learning need lots of sleep to process information.

Dogs are polyphasic sleepers, meaning they have multiple naps throughout the day and night. They also experience Rapid Eye Movement sleep (REM). Sometimes you may observe this REM when your dog's eyes move even though they are asleep. It is believed that REM part of the sleep is vital for memory build up.

Always provide your dog with different areas or types of bed to sleep in. Your dog needs somewhere to rest his head because he's frequently 'dog-tired'!

More about Diane

Diane is a Dog Trainer and Behaviour Consultant with her company Superhounds and is also co-author of "Beyond The Bowl" - a book about providing more mental stimulation for your pet dog.
She is also the co-founder of The Canine Revolution
www.superhounds.co.uk
www.thecaninerevolution.co.uk

The greatest gift you can give any dog is confidence

- Dr. Ian Dunbar

Ian Explains

Anxiety and fearfulness are crippling conditions. For example, if a dog is fearful of people, every day the dog is forced to confront its biggest nightmare — people! Trying to resolve fearfulness in an adult dog usually takes many months, or years and so, safely socialise your young puppy to people at home. Make sure to instruct all visitors to remove outdoor shoes before coming inside to prevent fomite transmission of parvovirus and distemper from faeces and urine on shoe soles.

More about Ian

Dr. Ian Dunbar is a veterinarian, animal behaviourist, dog trainer, author, lecturer, skier, gardener and Arsenal, Yorkshire and Warriors supporter. After retiring from the seminar trail (nine months a year in hotels), Dr. Dunbar now lectures online at <u>DunbarAcademy.com</u> and occasionally blogs and vlogs at <u>DogStarDaily.com</u>

Shift Focus; Work with your dog to achieve positive, desired behaviour together, rather than worrying about what your dog is doing wrong

- Jo Pay

Jo Explains

As humans, we find it very easy to be critical and focus on what our dogs are doing wrong, or what they can't do. Shift focus! Now, look at how we would like our dogs to behave and work towards that. We can then train our dogs more effectively, build strong bonds and enjoy a more positive relationship with our pets.

More about Jo

Jo runs Standish Dog Trainer in the North West of England. Jo is also the European Coordinator for Victoria Stilwell Positively Dog Training and is on the faculty of the Victoria Stilwell Academy.
Jo enjoys walking and training her two border collies, Indie and Twist.
www.standishdogtrainer.co.uk
www.jopay.co.uk

Learn when to STAY and when to WALK AWAY

- Justine Schuurmans

Justine Explains

This is a crucial lesson to help keep children safe
around the dogs they know, love and live with.

Being able to read situations and a dog's body
language helps to answer this all-important
question of when to stay and when to walk away.

More about Justine

Justine Schuurmans is the owner of The Family Dog,
an online training company for the WHOLE family.

The company's fun, music-based videos for
kids have quickly become the trademark of all their
online programs. With in-school training programs
and an international bite prevention campaign, the
company's mission is to help families worldwide live
happily and safely with their dogs.
www.thefamilydog.com

Use it or lose it!

– Karen Bush

Karen Explains

Any skill needs regular practice to keep it sharp - so keep working on the old and familiar behaviours such as 'sit' as well as teaching new ones. Make sure you keep it fun for both of you and rewarding for your dog, even if it is for doing something very simple. There is evidence that in addition to enrichment toys, training can help slow the onset of CCD (aka Doggy Dementia) which is another good reason for keeping it up!

More about Karen

Karen has been a regular contributor to Your Dog Magazine since 1985. She has written several books including The Dog Expert, Dog-friendly Gardening, Haunting Hounds, and recently co-authored a series of mini-titles with Toni Shelbourne covering common canine issues such as firework fear and car travel. www.karenbush.jimdo.com
www.dogfriendlygardening.jimdo.com
www.tonishelbournendkarenbush.jimdo.com

A dog should compliment your life, not complicate it!

- Kay Attwood

Kay Explains

Having a dog should be pleasurable and not change your life to the point of complicating it. Dogs are very adaptable. Don't make life complicated, make it simple and enjoyable. Make your training simple - make your ownership simple. Relax and enjoy your dog.

More about Kay

Dog trainer and Behaviourist with many years experience. Teaching dog owners and dog trainers all over the world. Www.kay9service.co.uk

It's Just Information

- Lynda Taylor

Lynda Explains

You've worked hard at training that recall or loose lead walking and then all of a sudden, maybe in the park, it disappears. You call your dog and he heads into the distance or he suddenly flies to the end of the lead, pulling hard. Those moments can be frustrating and disheartening but in reality...it's just information. It's the kind of information which tells you that when children are playing with a ball, it's too distracting to come when called. It's information that when a cyclist goes by, it's too exciting to keep a loose lead.

The great thing? You now have more information about your dog's understanding of the behaviour. Now you can create a plan which teaches your dog how to maintain focus whilst children play with balls or cyclists zoom past. Now you know the limitations of your dog's understanding you can set them up for success.

More about Lynda

Lynda Taylor has been involved in dog training and behaviour for over 25 years and is a director of www.positiveanimalsolutions.com and www.performancedog.co.uk
She is a lecturer on degree courses in canine behaviour and training at Bishop Burton College and provides behavioural support for the dogs cared for at www.galgosdelsol.org.

There is no such thing as easy ways to train, just as there was never an idiot's guide to rearing children. Unless of course, you want to rear idiots

– Kay Laurence

Kay Explains

Be wary, very wary of promises of easy training and easy solutions. The fast and dirty methods have a high price to pay and that price is usually paid by the learner, not the teacher. Learning should always be a positive experience because it lasts for life, not just for the moment.

More about Kay

Kay Laurence
Sharing life managed by collies in a style demanded by Gordon Setters.
Innovative and effective teaching by learning about dogs. Training based on science and understanding, delivered with experience and empathy, reinforced from the heart with passion, joy and enthusiasm.
Learningaboutdogs.com

If you exercise your dog every day until he is physically tired, you are creating an athlete

— Lily Clark

Lily Explains

Similar to going to the gym, the more exerise you do, the stronger your body becomes until the original amount is no longer sufficient to tire you out. The more exercise you give your dog, the harder it will be to physically tire him and the more he will expect. Teach your dogs tricks and give them games and puzzles to engage in. This will tire your dog out mentally and engage their problem-solving skills.

More about Lily

Lily created Suppawt as a bespoke service providing realistic training for normal people and normal dogs. Lily specializes in rehabilitating rescue and reactive dogs.
BSc Hons Animal Behaviour, APDT
www.suppawt.com

*Train your dog as you
would like to be trained
yourself*

- Sally Marchant

Sally Explains

Imagine that you are being trained by an alien who doesn't understand your language. Ask yourself if you like the chosen training method? If the answer is no - then consider another method to train your dog where the answer is yes. Our dogs can and should look forward to training.

More about Sally

Sally Marchant runs www.naturallyhappydogs.com, the online video library with answers to all of your canine questions, all as short, easy to watch videos. Sign up for a month for free using the code HTNOMENO.
Sally also runs www.dog-and-bone.co.uk, running seminars for dog professionals.

Dogs don't think we're dogs

- Lisa Tenzin-Dolma

Lisa Explains

Dogs form social groups, rather than packs and they understand that we're humans, not dogs and relate to us accordingly. They have no desire to become 'pack leader', so the old way of thinking that we must be 'alpha', or our dogs will rule the roost with an iron paw, is a fallacy.

Our dogs view us as their beloved companions. All they ask of us is that we treat them considerately and with respect for their doggy natures, meet their physical, emotional and mental needs and take the time to ensure they understand what we're asking of them.

More about Lisa

Lisa Tenzin-Dolma is founder and principal of The International School for Canine Psychology & Behaviour, founder of The Dog Welfare Alliance and co-chair of The Association of INTODogs. She represents INTODogs within the Animal Behaviour & Training Council. Lisa has had 33 books published, including five about dog behaviour.
www.theiscp.com

Clarity begins at home

- Sarah Fisher

Sarah Explains

The way we handle dogs can be the trigger for some of the behaviours we wish to modify or change. Ruffling a dog's ears or coat, patting, and hurried interactions can increase arousal and concern.

Many dogs described as 'enthusiastic' greeters or those that hang back are actually touch sensitive and carry tension or discomfort in the body.

Slowing down handling and becoming mindful of the dog's nervous system responses as you stroke them gently can give you vital information about your canine friend.

Pay attention to their rate of respiration, blink rate, any increase or decrease of movement through the body (including the tail). Note if they turn their head, step away, roll over, pant, gulp or sneeze. Look for alterations in the texture and appearance of the coat; swirls, dandruff, coarse or fluffy areas, and body sensitivity can be an indicator of skeletal change or soft tissue injury/tension.

More about Sarah

Sarah Fisher is Tellilngton TTouch Instructor. TTouch is an integrated approach for animal handling, education and rehabilitation. TTouch recognises an inextricable link between posture and behaviour and combines observations, body work and ground work exercises to improve physical, mental and emotional well-being. www.ttouch.co.uk

Ask not what your dog
can do for you - ask what
you can do for your
dog. (To paraphrase John
F. Kennedy)

- Sue Kinchin

Sue Explains

Too often the relationship between a dog and its owner is marred because the owner wants their dog to fulfil a personal ideal or ambition. Disappointment is often shown in phrases like "I wanted to do agility, but my dog doesn't like queuing with other dogs.", "I wanted a dog to take for local walks, but he doesn't like traffic.", "I want my dog to play with other dogs, but he doesn't like them.".

We are already making huge demands on another species in asking a dog to live alongside us without also asking our dog to fulfil our dreams. Each dog has its own personality and preferences and we should appreciate and honour each dog for who he or she is.
Find out what your particular dog likes and make that the activity you enjoy together, even if it's not what you first had in mind.

More about Sue

Sue Kinchin has been training her own and other people's dogs for 55 years. This has meant the continual study of canine behaviour and training methods to remain up-to-date. An APDT UK member for many years, Sue has now retired to concentrate on sharing her knowledge through writing.

WTF?

- Susan G. Friedman

Susan Explains

No matter where in the world I am teaching or what language is spoken there, everyone laughs heartily when this acronym comes up. I have to quickly explain that in this case, WTF has a very different and important meaning: What's the function? In other words, what outcome or consequence does the behavior of interest produce? When we answer that question, we better understand why dogs behave the way they do. Outcomes give our behavior function.

More about Susan

Dr. Friedman is a retired psychology professor who consults with animal caregivers around the world. She disseminates the science of behavior change and its effective, humane teaching technology, applied behavior analysis. Her website has articles, posters and other media (including translations), which is available for downloading, free of charge. www.behaviorworks.org

The Reliable Recall is the most essential piece of the human-canine bond

– Tracie Hotchner

Tracie Explains

Teaching a dog to return to you joyfully and speedily no matter what the circumstances is a fundamental piece of attachment and communication. It shows the dog's eager acceptance of you as benevolently in charge and eliminates many awkward as well as dangerous situations. You can recognize a solid and mutually respectful relationship when you see a dog rushing back to his person at the sound of his name and the words "Come" or "Here" called out with cheerful confidence.

More about Tracie

Author of "The Dog Bible: Everything Your Dog Wants You to Know," host/producer of the long-running NPR radio show DOG TALK, as well as 8 other pet talk podcasts (including the training show GOOD DOGS!) and director of the NY Dog Film Festival, now in its 3rd year.
http://www.radiopetlady.com

Teaching happens when the teacher is talking. Learning happens when the teacher is quiet

– Theresa McKeon

Editors Comments

Whilst this excellent phrase is primarily aimed at teaching people, it is worth remembering that every dog owner is a teacher/trainer and every pet dog, a learner. Also, all species learn similarly.

Theresa Explains

There is a belief that lots of talking means lots of learning. It may be that learning happens despite all the talking.
• If there is a need to constantly repeat instructions or encouragement while a student is acquiring a behavior, the behavior may be too long.
• Break the behavior into smaller parts which can be taught with a minimum of verbal language.
• The student will build (self) confidence in each of the components, and eventually in the final compound behavior.
• Student self-sufficiency is built right into your teaching plan, which is every teacher's goal.

More about Theresa

Theresa (Co-founder TAGteach International) was a national level gymnastic coach determined to find a way to speed up skill acquisition for her athletes. Her search for behaviorally sound techniques and clean instructions led to the development of the TAGteach methodology. Theresa now consults for corporations, hospitals and in industrial settings. www.tagteach.com

Just because you can,
doesn't mean you should

– Val Harvey

Val Explains

It is very easy to move puppies and small dogs into the position you want, e.g. pulling them back if they pull on their lead, pulling them away from rubbish or an interesting smell. But just because you can, doesn't mean you should.

The dog doesn't learn anything by being pulled (except how uncomfortable it is to be on a lead). It is much better to train them to walk on a loose lead, to 'leave it' when asked or to let them have a quick sniff before asking them to walk on, etc. It is important that your dog understands how to follow instructions whether on lead or not.

The same applies to handling, getting a dog into a Sit or Down etc. – Please help your dog understand what is required using reward-based training and don't be tempted to use force. Just because you can, doesn't mean you should!

More about Val

Val has been helping people to train their dogs for more than twenty years. She is a member of APDT, UK whose members coach owners to train their dogs using kind, fair and effective methods. Details of the Association of Pet Dog Trainers can be found on www.apdt.co.uk

The pup is parent of the dog

- Dr. Ian Dunbar

Ian Explains

Good dogs are made in puppyhood. Puppy brains are extremely receptive and have a high degree of plasticity and so, may easily and quickly be shaped and molded to your liking, especially in terms of behavior, activity level, personality, confidence and temperament. To attempt to do the same in adulthood would take months and maybe years and yet, the adult dog will never be what it could have been.

More about Ian

Dr. Ian Dunbar is a veterinarian, animal behaviourist, dog trainer, author, lecturer, skier, gardener and Arsenal, Yorkshire and Warriors supporter. After retiring from the seminar trail (nine months a year in hotels), Dr. Dunbar now lectures online at DunbarAcademy.com and occasionally blogs and vlogs at DogStarDaily.com

A dog in a kennel barks at his fleas — a dog out hunting does not even notice them
(Old Chinese proverb)

- Tony Cruse

Tony Explains

This proverb makes the point that active exercise and stimulation enriches and provides the dog with a healthy outlet. A bored dog may find a way of coping by chewing or barking at the tiniest of irritations or smallest changes within the environment.

Giving your dog a chance to run and use his nose is tapping into his natural behaviours of hunting and scavenging. Walks and the opportunity to sniff are very necessary for the pet dog. Many dogs exhibit unwanted behaviours such as barking and jumping up due to a lack of enrichment. They are bored and unfulfilled. By adding a daily scentwork exercise or simply 'scatter feeding', you can easily give him a rewarding task and improve the life of your pet dog... and the family!

More about Tony

Tony Cruse is a full-time dog trainer who also advises on a variety of canine problem behaviours. He often runs scentwork activities in Essex, UK called, 'Hide & Scent'. Tony is the creator of this very book. His last book was the highly regarded. '101 Doggy Dilemmas'.
www.tc-dog-training.co.uk

If you're not training the dog, the dog is training you!

– Donna Saunders

Donna Explains

Anywhere & everywhere - learning is always happening even when resting (e.g. when you're sitting watching TV and the dog is doing great lying on the floor not trashing the house or chewing on your leg - tell him he's doing great don't just ignore!)

Be aware of what you are reinforcing!

More about Donna

Donna owns In The Doghouse Pet Lodge & Training Centre in Spain & has many hats!

Donna has been working with dogs for 11 years and has picked up amongst others, City & Guilds, IMDT & FitPaws accreditations along her journey.
www.inthedoghousedtc.com

It's a puppy; not a problem!

– Denise Fenzi

Denise Explains

Puppies are challenging! They have a big job ahead of them learning how to get along in our human world. Our job is to recognize where we want to go with their behavior and slowly mold them in that direction.

There is nothing wrong or abnormal about a puppy expressing normal puppy behaviors such as digging, chewing, barking, etc., even if we find it annoying. If we can learn to accept our young puppies the way we accept our young children, the odds are good that we can maintain our perspective and sense of humor throughout that first challenging year or two. Eventually, we'll end up with the beautifully trained companion we had always wished for.

More about Denise

Denise is a professional dog trainer who specializes in motivation and preparing dog sports teams for competition using no-force training methods. Her books can be found on Amazon worldwide. Denise's online school can be found at www.fenzidogsportsacademy.com

What gets rewarded, gets repeated

- Hannah Wilkinson

Hannah Explains

Dogs have evolved over the years to live in our busy world and are constantly trying out new behaviours. If these behaviours get the desired outcome, our dogs learn to repeat them. For example, if a dog runs off with the remote control and is given chase, he learns that it's a fun game and will likely repeat the behaviour of picking up items and running off with them! Equally, if we use food to reward him when he checks in on us, this behaviour is also likely to be repeated.

It is also worth noting that rewards can come in any form and are individual to each dog. For example, a Labrador may love a piece of chicken, a Spaniel may love sniffing, whereas just making eye contact with a Staffordshire Bull Terrier can be rewarding enough to send him into a tail wagging frenzy!

More about Hannah

Hannah Wilkinson (BA (Hons) CertHE) has been involved in dog training for over 15 years, she is a member of the APDT UK, a Kennel Club Accredited Trainer, a Tellington Ttouch practitioner and can currently be found running fun dog training classes. www.spektrumk9.com

Know the normal, treat the abnormal

– Annie Phenix, CPDT-KA

Annie Explains

I first heard this term from veterinary behaviorist, Dr Soraya Juarbe-Diaz, who was speaking at a Florida, USA dog industry conference and I've never forgotten it. It is our responsibility as dog owners and trainers to understand enough about canine behavior to know what is normal behavior and what is abnormal. Normal behavior we shape, guide and positively train as we communicate to dogs what behavior we desire from them. Abnormal behavior most often requires professional help.

Normal: Puppies chew as they teethe.

Abnormal: Puppy grows out of puppy-dom and continues excessively chewing on everything and anything, sometimes even chewing on their own feet, flanks or tails. Perhaps the dog has an abnormal amount of anxiety and needs help coping with that strong emotion. Maybe there is a health issue that a veterinarian needs to be involved. It might be related to something specific such as storm phobia. Investigation is warranted.

More about Annie

Annie Phenix, CPDT-KA is a registered Fear Free Trainer specializing in behavior cases. She is the author of the best selling book: The Midnight Dog Walkers: Positive Training and Practical Advice for Living with Reactive and Aggressive Dogs. Also, a columnist for Dogster Magazine. Based in Utah in the USA. www.phenixdogs.com

Fear is Sticky

- Tony Cruse

Tony Explains

This is a widely known phrase among professionals who work with reactive dogs. In nature, if an animal has cause to be scared, in future he will avoid the source of his fear and often everything that surrounded it. It makes good survival sense! The source has caused the fear to stick....be afraid of the rampaging elephants in that location!

Now, imagine if you accidentally drop a baking tin beside your dog in the kitchen. It could make him afraid so he avoids the kitchen... and possibly even you! Avoidance and sometimes growling can occur. Common fears are of the vet surgery, vehicles, other dogs etc.

To counter this 'sticky' fear, it can take multiple repetitions using positive associations. One quick, scary experience can take countless positive experiences to reverse. Your puppy/dog requires a history of pleasant experiences, so try not to expose him to potentially frightening situations.

More about Tony

Tony Cruse is a full-time dog trainer who also advises on a variety of canine problem behaviours. He is a regular feature writer for various magazines. A sought-after speaker, he is a nominated lecturer for Writtle College University, UK.
Tony is the producer of this very book.
www.tc-dog-training.co.uk

Good habits are just as
hard to break as bad
habits and so, teach your
puppy/dog good habits
from the outset

– Kelly Gorman Dunbar

Kelly Explains

Teach your puppy or newly adopted adult dog where to pee and poop, what to chew, where to dig, when to bark and when to jazz up and settle down (on cue) the first day it comes home.

More about Kelly

Kelly is the Vice President of the Center for Applied Behavior Inc and the executive Editor of DogStarDaily.com
www.dogstardaily.com

Did you know that he was a Terrier* when you adopted him?

– Linda Case

Linda Explains

*Note: Terrier can be replaced with any breed group, breed, or breed type. This statement refers to the very common belief by dog owners that an unwanted behavior shown by their dogs is "abnormal". In fact, the vast majority of undesirable behaviors in dogs are just normal dog (or breed-related) behaviors that humans find to be incompatible with our lifestyles. Terriers dig, retrievers carry stuff and herding breeds chase. Having an understanding of and respect for "dogs as dogs" is integral to effective training and to build a loving bond between an owner and their dog.

More about Linda

Linda Case is a dog trainer, canine nutritionist and science writer. She owns AutumnGold Consulting and Dog Training Center located in central Illinois, USA. Linda is the author of seven dog books and "The Science Dog" blog.
www.thesciencedog.wordpress.com

Don't get caught with your fingers in the till!

– Kay Attwood

Kay Explains

During training, when we put our hand in our treat bag too early, the dog can stop the behaviour midway in order to receive the treat. Therefore, don't put your hand in the bag until you are ready to pay the dog immediately.

More about Kay

Dog trainer and Behaviourist with many years experience. Teaching dog owners and dog trainers all over the world. Www.kay9service.co.uk

Dogs are emotional beings

- Lisa Tenzin-Dolma

Lisa Explains

Scientific studies have revealed that dogs experience a wide range of emotions, including happiness, sadness, fear, anxiety, grief, depression, anger, loneliness, empathy, and love, and that they process emotions in the same areas of the brain as we do.

Our dogs are highly influenced by our emotional states and respond to these accordingly. Because of this, it makes sense to be aware of what we are feeling and to understand how this affects our relationships with our dogs.

More about Lisa

Lisa Tenzin-Dolma is founder and principal of The International School for Canine Psychology & Behaviour, founder of The Dog Welfare Alliance, and co-chair of The Association of INTODogs. She represents INTODogs within the Animal Behaviour & Training Council. Lisa has had 33 books published, including five about dog behaviour. www.theiscp.com.

Step 1: Don't follow the steps!

- Silvia Trkman

Silvia Explains

Dogs are not machines, so they don't come with instructions and there is no one best way that would work for all. Listen to the dog you have, adjust, be flexible and creative, think out of the box and always remember it's not the best dog that wins. - It's the best team that wins. So what your dog thinks about you is way more important as what other people think about your dog.

More about Silvia

Silvia Trkman is one of the most successful agility competitors and trainers, winning World, European and National Championships many times with various dogs for past 20 years. www.lolabuland.com

Prepare, Don't Despair

- Toni Shelbourne

Toni Explains

I like to pre-empt any problems by being proactive. That might be teaching my dog that a bicycle means, return for a treat and calmly watch it go by. Or starting Tellington TTouch body work a month early to prepare him for the firework season. My point is, if we aim for success, the off-shoot benefit is we keep our dogs safe, confident and compliant in the real world. We have a duty to coach our dogs in the skills they require to fit into our confusing world so they can be stress-free and emotionally content.

More about Toni

Toni Shelbourne has worked professionally with dogs since 1989. She is a Tellington TTouch Practitioner, Real Dog Yoga Instructor and Author. Visit www.tonishelbourne.co.uk to find out more. For the 'HELP! My Dog...' book series, visit the Facebook page. Canine EBooks by Toni Shelbourne & Karen Bush (Also available in paperback).

Feeding only from Kongs is the easiest way to reprogramme your dog's brain in the shortest amount of time

– Dr. Ian Dunbar

Ian Explains

When dogs eat from hollow chewtoys, they usually lie down. Each piece of food the dog extricates from the Kong rewards the dog for lying down, quietly and calmly, i.e. for NOT running around and barking. Additionally, Kong-feeding gives the dog a hobby to help wile away the hours when left at home alone, i.e., prevents or resolves separation anxiety.

Feeding from bowls is physically and psychologically unhealthy. It is unnatural for a dog's stomach to be distended on a regular basis each day. Moreover, bowl-feeding steals the dog's raison d'être. When left to their own devices, most dogs would spend their waking hours sniffing and searching for scraps to eat. Kong-feeding enables dogs to enjoy their day nibbling at food.

More about Ian

Dr. Ian Dunbar is a veterinarian, animal behaviourist, dog trainer, author, lecturer, skier, gardener and Arsenal, Yorkshire and Warriors supporter. After retiring from the seminar trail (nine months a year in hotels), Dr. Dunbar now lectures online at DunbarAcademy.com and occasionally blogs and vlogs at DogStarDaily.com

It depends...

– Suzanne Clothier

Suzanne Explains

Dog owners would love to have clear-cut answers to their problems or concerns. Why does my dog bark? Why did my dog bite? How do I make him ignore squirrels? Why [fill in the blank]? Finding out what's what requires good detective work, because "it depends..." reflects the complexity of the possible causes & solutions that may be behind a dog's behavior.

Something as simple as, "My dog won't sit" can be due to many factors: a) doesn't know SIT; b) excitement; c) has back or knee issues; d) confusion; e) fear; f) slippery surface; g) mixed signals; h) too hot/cold/wet/rough, etc.

The art of training lies in knowing how and what to search for while seeking understanding and appropriate answers for that individual dog. Buffy cannot sit if she's excited, Tyler won't sit because of arthritic knees. Calming Buffy and respecting Tyler come from understanding that "it depends..."

About Suzanne

Trainer Suzanne Clothier's Relationship Centered Training (RCT) approach has helped countless dogs worldwide with her innovative, humane techniques. The author of the highly regarded "Bones Would Rain from the Sky", she has developed a broad range of programs for dog lovers, trainers & organizations (CARAT, RAT, FAT, Enriched Puppy). www.suzanneclothier.com

Behavior is a study of one

- Susan G. Friedman

Susan Explains

Regardless of breed norms and generalizations, when working with a particular dog, that dog is an individual, with it's own unique "culture" and "customs." In this way, our universal principles of behavior are custom to fit the individual learner.

More about Susan

Dr. Friedman is a retired psychology professor who consults with animal caregivers around the world. She disseminates the science of behavior change and its effective, humane teaching technology, applied behavior analysis. Her website has articles, posters and other media (including translations), which is available for downloading, free of charge. www.behaviorworks.org

Learning Shouldn't Hurt

- Linda Michaels, M.A., Psychology

Linda Explains

"Learning Shouldn't Hurt" seems like a no-brainer. Sadly, in reality, the state of the dog training "industry" and the popularity of shock, prong, and choke collars, and dominance and punitive methods being promoted and normalized as feasible options to train our pet dogs, mandates that we shout it from the rooftops loud and clear.

We call on: Every dog-loving citizen to monitor how their government representatives vote on animal welfare issues, our legislators to strengthen our animal welfare laws and to increase and enforce penalties for animal abuse and neglect, the community of dog-loving pet parents to open their eyes to the fact that the field of dog training is entirely unregulated and to not follow instructions from anyone to hurt their dogs and our field to embed a "Do No Harm" ethical principle into training. Only then can we regulate trainers to a standard of professional competence.

More about Linda

Linda Michaels, M.A., Psychology, author of "Do No Harm" Dog Training, is the creator of the HierarchyOfDogNeeds.com infographic used by veterinary behaviorists and trainers. Linda's research experience in behavioral neurobiology makes her an expert in training aggressive dogs, puppies and wolfdogs in the Del Mar, CA area of the USA. DogPsychologistOnCall.com

Imagine your dog is not wearing a collar or lead. How are you going to train him now?

– Tim Bleecker

Tim Explains

As owners, we often forget that leads and collars take away a fundamental choice a dog should have, which is the ability to move away or take another necessary option.
Inappropriate use of leads/collars can and do influence the relationship between owner and dog (think lead yank/leash pop).
If we had to train with no lead/collar, we'd have to work harder but the result would be that we would learn much more.

More about Tim

Tim runs classes in Nottingham/Mansfield, UK and carries out 1-2-1 sessions assisting owners with behavioural issues.
He takes a special interest in helping owners understand and deal with dog-to-dog aggression.

Tim is a full member of the
Association of Pet Dog Trainers, (APDT UK)
www.nottinghamdogtrainer.co.uk
www.mansfielddogtraining.co.uk

Feed Fido on Fact not Fashion

- Jacqueline Boyd

Jacqueline Explains

Feeding your dog well should be based on robust scientific fact AND what works for you and your dog; not what is fashionable or what some celebrity feeds their dog. Key points to identify in choosing a food and feeding strategy; your budget, your time, your dog (age, sex, size, activity level, health etc.), your ethical and moral views (perhaps relating to issues like sustainability or sourcing of ingredients). Consider your dog and your situation on an individual basis and experiment until you find a feeding strategy that works for all. Do not make huge or multiple dietary changes over a short time period and never feel pressurised to change if what you are doing works for you and your dog.

More about Jacqueline

Dr Jacqueline Boyd is a university lecturer in Animal Science, teaching a range of canine-related subjects from genetics to nutrition. She is passionate about using science and education to improve canine health and welfare.
jacqueline.boyd@ntu.ac.uk

"But he shouldn't
growl at me"
Your dog should have no
need to growl at you

- Tony Cruse

Tony Explains

I often hear owners questioning why their dog has the 'front' to growl at them as if they were being challenged. However, if we consider a growl is often the result of fear, we must ask why the dog was in a situation where he felt the need to growl. A social and confident dog has no need to growl. He has been taught from puppyhood that food is plentiful, toys are plentiful and that strange hat... is just a hat! His owner will not steal his food. Actually, his owner provides his food. No need for anxious warnings there!

If your dog growls at you calmly step back and consider why your dog felt worried enough to growl. Later, you can work on prevention or rebuilding his confidence in that situation.

More about Tony

Tony Cruse is a full-time dog trainer who also advises on a variety of canine problem behaviours. He has completed over 900 training and behaviour consultations. Tony is also a writer and a sought-after speaker.
Tony is the producer of this very book.
www.tc-dog-training.co.uk

It has long been agreed that animals do not belong in a circus, so why do we create a domestic circus for dogs? They deserve far more respect than that

– Isla Fishburn

Isla Explains

There is a lack of recognition among many about how complex our dogs are and what they are always in need of. Dogs are learning, observing and absorbing information all of the time. Yet, many dogs are so often placed in situations, homes or environments where they are made to perform, be controlled, commanded or coerced to do things that the dog is not comfortable in doing or goes against their wishes.

I consider this nothing more than slavery and imprisonment. Dogs have a spirit, a joy and a desire that they should be encouraged to express. This can quickly be extinguished by human guardians, especially when we do not recognise the difference between a dog interacting and engaging because of the pleasure it brings, against a dog being made to perform. The former promotes canine health and wellness, whilst the latter impedes it.

More about Isla

Dr Fishburn has had a long interest in nature, healing and conservation. After spending several years with captive wolves and learning more about wellness, Isla began to observe the many distresses that domestic dogs experience. Isla created Kachina Canine to provide support for dogs and to educate their human guardians. www.kachinacanine.com

Protect your dog so he doesn't have to protect himself!

– Justine Schuurmans

Justine Explains

This is to encourage parents to really take the time to learn how to read their dog's body language AND then to take action by stepping in to help when he's struggling.

If a dog feels protected by the parents - they will always look to them to resolve a tricky situation rather than taking matters into their own hands/teeth!!

More about Justine

Justine Schuurmans is the owner of The Family Dog, an online training company for the WHOLE family. The company's fun, music-based videos for kids have quickly become the trademark of all their online programs. With in-school training programs and an international bite prevention campaign, the company's mission is to help families worldwide live happily and safely with their dogs. www.thefamilydog.com

It's not Hocus-Pocus! It's simply about teaching our dogs Focus

– Mik Moeller

Mik Explains

We do not need a magic wand nor are there any magic potions –it's simply about reinforcing our dogs to focus on us. The more we reinforce the behaviors we want, the more the dog will start to offer them. Without any focus, training is almost impossible.

More about Mik

Mik Moeller has been involved in canine behavior for almost 20 years and his passion is working in the animal shelter industry. He is the author of 'Reactive Rover- an owners guide to on-leash dog aggression'.
www.moellerdog.com

Kindness and consistency are the keys to successful dog training

– Jane Williams

Jane Explains

Dogs look to us humans for guidance about their behaviour. We have a responsibility as owners to guide them towards desirable behaviours. The best way method dog is through reward-based training. To train dogs effectively requires kindness - that means sticking to a reward-based approach. It doesn't mean letting dogs do as they want all of the time. It means asking them to show good behaviours and rewarding them for doing as we ask. Examples would include sitting when greeting a visitor at home or on the walk; or releasing a ball to us when it has been retrieved. When we ask dogs to do things, we need to be as consistent as we can - try to use the same words and the same hand signals every time, that way the dog learns quickly.

More about Jane

Jane Williams has been involved in animal training and behaviour for twenty years. She is a full member of the APBC (since 2017, the Chair), the APDT UK and the BVBA. She is a Certified Clinical Animal Behaviourist and is ABTC listed. Jane lives with numerous rescued dogs, rabbits and tortoises.

choice gives a dog confidence

- Lily Clark

Lily Explains

If the dog you are working with understands he can leave the situation any time he is uncomfortable, he is much more likely to try new things. Whereas, a dog which is forced into situations or interactions soon becomes anxious and less likely to trust their handler's judgement. If you push, they will push back.

More about Lily

Lily created Suppawt as a bespoke service providing realistic training for normal people and normal dogs. Lily specializes in rehabilitating rescue and reactive dogs.
BSc Hons Animal Behaviour, APDT.
www.suppawt.com

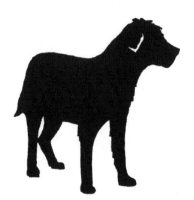

There is no such thing as 'bad' behaviour

- Kirsten Dillon

Kirsten Explains

There is NO SUCH THING as naughty or bad behaviour from your dog. Yes, you read this correctly. There is no 'right' or 'wrong' in a dog's world, no 'good' or 'naughty', there is simply 'safe' and 'unsafe' and in our world 'wanted' and 'unwanted' behaviours.

If your dog steals food from the counter, that isn't naughty, its natural foraging behaviour, a very useful skill for a dog. It may be unwanted, but it isn't naughty. If your dog won't come back, that isn't bad behaviour either, if you haven't taught your dog to recall, how is he supposed to know?

Therefore, NEVER punish behaviours you don't want, as they are perfectly reasonable in our dog's minds. Simply interrupt them and show your dog what you would like him to do instead.

You can call your dog 'untrained' or 'unmotivated', just please don't call him 'bad' for doing what dogs do.

More about Kirsten

Kirsten Dillon is a dog trainer and behaviourist, working in Surrey and London, UK. She is also Head of Training at the charity Veterans With Dogs and a Trainer and Assessor for Dog AID (Assistance In Disability).www.kdcaninespecialist.com

Any behaviour that is reinforced/rewarded will be repeated

– Val Harvey

Val Explains

We often hear of a dog doing something the owner doesn't like and they can't work out why the dog doesn't understand 'NO' in these circumstances. It is always worth looking at what is sustaining the behaviour – remember that any behaviour that is reinforced will be repeated. Dog takes a teatowel, owner chases him to get it back. The dog has been rewarded by a game of chase or tug. Dog is bored, starts barking, owner asks (or shouts) him to be quiet. The dog has been rewarded by gaining attention. The dog jumps up. He is told 'NO' or pushed away. The dog has received attention and been rewarded.

Instead, train your dog not to jump up, teach him a 'drop' but most of all, don't expect him not to get bored. Training, playing and interactive /puzzle games will help prevent a myriad of problems.

More about Val

Val has been helping people to train their dogs for more than twenty years. She is a member of APDT, UK whose members coach owners to train their dogs using kind, fair and effective methods. Members can be found on www.apdt.co.uk

Persistence is Futile - Do Less for Success!

- Anna Patfield

<u>Anna Explains</u>

Einstein probably wasn't thinking about dog behaviour when he coined the phrase, 'Insanity is doing the same thing over and over again and expecting different results'. But the sentiment is valid.
Avoidance of failure is a crucially important aspect with regard to successfully changing a dog's behaviour. We will achieve much more by taking tiny successful steps than by creating situations where the dog continues to fail. For instance: teach heel one step at a time, teach down one inch at a time, teach calmness at a distance and just for a moment. Then build on those successes. Exposing our dogs again and again to situations that create an undesirable behaviour simply serves to build or maintain that habit.
Break the habit by changing the circumstances.

<u>More about Anna</u>

Anna is a fully qualified and experienced dog behaviourist with a passion for unravelling the mysteries surrounding behaviour and behavioural nutrition. She can help you to get inside your dog's mind and to really understand what makes them tick.
PawsAbility.co.uk
TheGoodDogDiet.com

We should not be trying
change dogs.
We should be trying to
change the world in
which they live

– Kay Laurence

<u>Kay Explains</u>

Dogs are exceptional because they are dogs. The doggy things they enjoy can make us smile, laugh and love living with them. Some of their habits take a good deal of patience to adapt to house living, such as rolling in fox-poo or knocking the coffee cup flying. But we should not be trying to stop them being them, just learn how to live together and maybe adapt our lives, the way we live, and most importantly the way we see their behaviour.
There are no bad dogs, just wrong environments. Change the environment and the dog will work hard to meet us halfway.

<u>More about Kay</u>

Kay Laurence
Sharing life managed by collies in a style demanded by Gordon Setters.
Innovative and effective teaching by learning about dogs. Training based on science and understanding, delivered with experience and empathy, reinforced from the heart with passion, joy and enthusiasm. <u>Learningaboutdogs.com</u>

Six feet of leash is a privilege, not a right

- Dawn Antoniak-Mitchell, Esq.
CPDT-KSA, CBCC-KA

Dawn Explains

When your dog is walking out at the end of his leash, problem behaviors are nearly impossible to prevent and teaching appropriate behaviors is very challenging. Pulling, inappropriate approaches towards people and dogs, and chase behaviors are all nearly impossible to change if your dog is six feet or more away from you.

Shorten up his leash and walk him closer to you while he is learning to walk politely on leash. Once he has mastered walking on a loose leash and politely passing other dogs and people, he can start enjoying the privilege of a bit more leash while out walking the neighborhood.

More about Dawn

Dawn has been training people and dogs for over twenty-five years. She has written several breed-focused training books, including the award-winning "Teach Your Herding Breed to be a Great Companion Dog: From Obsessive to Outstanding." She owns BonaFide Dog Academy in Omaha, NE, USA.
.www.bonafidedogacademy.com

You can't change any behaviour unless you change the emotion that drives it

– Carolyn Menteith

<u>Carolyn Explains</u>

Behaviours don't just 'happen'... Everything a dog does is a result of the way he feels. Change the way he feels and you change the behaviour.

Not only that but virtually every behaviour has a purpose and generally, that purpose is to make the dog feel better - to make bad stuff stop or go away.

If we want to improve a dog's behaviour we need to stop looking at the dog and thinking "how can I stop you from doing that thing that I don't like?" but instead we need to think "how can I make you feel better in this situation (or prevent the situation from occurring), so you don't need to do that thing which I don't like?".

It's only when we do that, can we work in an emotional partnership with our dogs and not in a dictatorship!

<u>More about Carolyn</u>

Carolyn is a trainer and behaviourist and has been working with dogs for the past 20 years. She has written several books, regular articles for Your Dog magazine, and specialises in improving the relationship between people and the dogs that share their lives. www.dogtalk.co.uk

"He only wants to play!"

- Karen Bush

Karen Explains

Unfortunately, other dogs you meet may not feel the same way! Some may react defensively if approached and this could set their training back and possibly result in injury to your dog. The experience could also traumatise him sufficiently to make him reactive too! So no matter how friendly he is, put your dog on a short fixed lead and check with the other owner before allowing a polite and controlled introduction to take place.

More about Karen

Karen has been a regular contributor to Your Dog Magazine since 1985. She has written over 20 books including The Dog Expert, Haunting Hounds, Dog-friendly Gardening, and is co-author with Toni Shelbourne of the 'Help! My Dog ...' mini-titles dealing with issues including firework fear and car travel.

www.karenbush.jimdo.com

A Dog's Nose Knows

- Louise Wilson

Louise Explains

On many occasions, I have to clarify that we need to "trust the dog" because the dog's nose knows. There is little need to question a dog's indication or a dog's reaction in a search area because they possess 300 million scent receptors, which by-far outnumbers our 5 million! They don't just detect an odour, they detect every particle of the odour! The dog's scent library and emotional connection with the scent, when properly trained, will bypass any other method of detection! Nothing (yet) is as effective! The Dog's Nose Knows!

More about Louise

As an expert detection dog trainer for conservation and law enforcement, Louise spends her days working with dogs and clients worldwide training new handlers in scentwork for fun workshops or operational searches!
Www.conservationk9consultancy.com

The most important rule is... have fun!

– Sally Marchant

Sally Explains

Dog training is a necessity that is most effective when enjoyed by both parties. If you find yourself getting stressed - take a break and come back to it later.

Only ever train your dog in a way that you would enjoy being trained by someone else.

If either of you are not enjoying the training you are doing, find a local dog trainer or online source of information to help you tweak and brighten up your training.

More about Sally

Sally Marchant runs www.naturallyhappydogs.com, the online video library with answers to all of your canine questions, all as short, easy to watch videos. Sign up for a month for free using the code HTNOMENO.
Sally also runs www.dog-and-bone.co.uk, running seminars for dog professionals.

Never Stop Learning!

- Tony Cruse

<u>Tony Explains</u>

Regardless of age or experience, we should never stop seeking out new information. Science is constantly evolving and changing. Whether a pet dog owner or a professional, we are all responsible for the future of the domestic dog. It is, therefore, our duty to keep on learning, progressing and developing.

Read dog books, dog magazines and attend talks about dogs! Seek out information and have fun learning! Please enjoy this book, keep it handy, spread the information and we can all learn something new. Our dogs can only benefit!

For more great canine information, please look up...

Andrea Arden, Anna Patfield, Annie Phenix, Carolyn Menteith, Claudia Estanislau, David Ryan, Dawn Antoniak-Mitchell, Denise Armstrong, Denise Fenzi, Diane Kasperowicz, Donna Saunders, Dr Ian Dunbar, Grisha Stewart, Hannah Wilkinson, Isla Fishburn, Jacqueline Boyd, Jane Arden, Jane Williams, Jean Donaldson, Jo Pay, Justine Schuurmans, Karen Bush, Kay Attwood, Kay Laurence, Kelly Gorman Dunbar, Kirsten Dillon, Lily Clark, Linda Case, Linda Michaels, Lisa Tenzin-Dolma, Louise Glazebrook, Louise Wilson, Lynda Taylor, Mik Moeller, Muriel Brasseur, Sally Marchant, Sarah Fisher, Silvia Trkman, Sue Kinchin, Susan G Friedman, Suzanne Clothier, Theresa McKeon, Tim Bleecker, Toni Shelbourne, Tony Cruse, Tracie Hotchner and Val Harvey.

About Woofs of Wisdom's Creator

Tony Cruse

UK Dog trainer and behavioural adviser, Tony Cruse has a wealth of experience helping owners to understand their dogs, improve their pet's behaviour and enjoy a successful relationship with their canine companion.

He is the owner and head trainer of Tc Dog Training, which incorporates a successful dog-training club called Galleywoofers. He also writes and speaks in all areas concerning canine behaviour and training.

Tony spends his free time watching cricket, live music (rock and jazz) and walking with Mötley (a Nova Scotia Duck Tolling Retriever) in the pleasant countryside of Galleywood, Essex, UK where he lives.

Also available by Tony Cruse

101 Doggy Dilemmas

Ever wondered, "Why does my dog do that?"

If so, help is at hand!

In 101 Doggy Dilemmas, you'll discover the reasons behind your dog's behaviour. Whether it's pulling on the lead, jumping up at people or hiding your shoes, this book will show positive strategies for dealing with those tricky training issues. You'll also discover how dogs think, learn and what really motivates your pet. It covers dogs and puppies and all breeds.

Based on the questions expert dog trainer Tony Cruse has been asked in his hundreds of dog training consultations and on his many radio appearances, this practical book provides a host of answers & advice to help you understand your canine companion better. A jargon-free promise, this book provides logical reasons and simple, do-able solutions to every-day canine issues.

Available on Amazon worldwide.

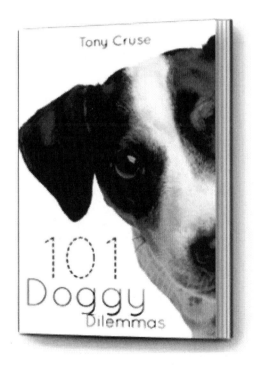

Tony Cruse

101
Doggy
Dilemmas

NOTES...

My Favourite Woofs...

Book Size 4.33" x 6" (10.998 x 15.24 cm)

Black & White on White paper

ISBN-13: 978-1976185984

ISBN-10: 197618598X

Made in the USA
San Bernardino, CA
26 April 2018